CASH FLOW

AN INVESTOR'S GUIDE TO FORECLOSED PROPERTY

How to Profit from Today's Foreclosure Market

LEARN HOW YOU CAN MAKE MONEY IN TODAY'S FORECLOSURE MARKET WITH THIS HANDY GUIDE. WITH OVER 30 YEARS' EXPERIENCE THE AUTHOR SHARES THE TIPS AND SECRETS THAT WILL SAVE YOU TIME AND SAVE YOU MONEY.

Henry Marshall Carner

CASH FLOW

AN INVESTOR'S GUIDE TO FORECLOSED PROPERTY

How to Profit from Today's Foreclosure Market

By
Henry Marshall Carner

Cash Flow

Investors Guide to Foreclosed Property

Copyright © 2011 Henry Marshall Carner

1st Edition

Cover design by Henry Marshall Carner

Edited by Ador Charming

Table of Contents

About the Author

Introduction

CHAPTER ONE: YOU THE INVESTOR, GETTING TO KNOW YOURSELF

CHAPTER TWO YOUR TOOLS

CHAPTER THREE THE GOALS

CHAPTER FOUR: THE PROPERTY SEARCH

CHAPTER FIVE: WHEN RENOVATING

CHAPTER SIX: A TYPICAL SCENARIO

Definition of terms

About the Author

Beginning as a tradesman in the early 1980's and having completed over 230 investor rehab projects in the last four years.

The author has extensive experience in the foreclosure market.

Most renovations have been single family homes for lease in Houston Texas.

In addition he has completed renovations for major retailers, hospitals, a few multi-family projects, and sports personalities.

Henry remains active today, investing and renovating in the Houston Texas area.

Introduction

The purpose of this guide is to provide a framework for investors who are interested in investing in single family rental property.

It will cover all aspects of the subject from acquisition through rental property management. Drawing upon extensive experience in the field, the author hopes this will be a most helpful tool. The author includes figures and real world examples as well as tips and secrets learned from 30 years' experience in the field.

CHAPTER ONE: YOU THE INVESTOR, GETTING TO KNOW YOURSELF

As you seek to define yourself as an investor you may ask yourself many questions. Am I comfortable with risk? Do I want to manage my properties? Or hire a manager? Do I like to make small repairs or will I contract someone to do them for me?

You may cross many mental boundaries during this process. I know I did. It took me awhile after doing several investment properties for others before I thought my self-ready to take the risk myself. You may be different able to assume the risk right away and be comfortable. You may be a tradesman, or a teacher a scientist or a musician.

The understanding of these tools will be the same.

First you may like to assemble a team, consisting of the following members:

1.   Realtor/ Agent this team member should be well versed in making offers on foreclosed properties. Verify this as foreclosures are a different animal.

2.   Accountant versed in tax advantages of rental property. You can also form an LLC to purchase properties in.

3.   Insurance agent will need to provide coverage while renovation is taking place as well as after tenant moves in. Pricing here can make a big difference in your cash flow!

4.   Property Manager needs to handle tenant screening, leases, evictions, and rent collection.

5.   General Contractor you may want to act as your own GC if repairs aren't to extensive. If they are make sure the GC has an understanding that this is a rental property portfolio and costs need to be kept as low as possible to provide the maximum return. Have him make sure all work is preformed to code.

6.   Property inspector will help determine if your target is suitable for investment or a lost cause.

7.   A final few words on team members. It is very important that you match up well with your team members and get along well with them, and they you. A good team will make for success; you will be relying on the integrity of your team members. Remember these are your investments were talking about and it is your money. Evaluate each team member on a performance basis and if one is failing, replace them.

CHAPTER TWO YOUR TOOLS

1.   Cash or cash equivalent. The no money days are pretty much over, to begin this process you will need some cash. We will cover a few of the ways to finance these properties in more detail. For right now, try to obtain some cash.

2.   Credit this aspect is more important than ever. We need to be conscious of our current credit situation and always working to improve it as well.

Good credit will give you access to more opportunities as you will be able to purchase more properties. Understand part of your credit picture is your debt to income ratio. This simply relates to how much you make verses how much you pay out each month in commitments. Obviously the lower the ratio is the better.

3.   Risk I am including risk as a tool simply because of the need for an investor to be comfortable with risk. All investing entails risk, we need to understand and mitigate this whenever possible. Used properly risks can equal reward. One way to help mitigate risk is to have your accountant form a corporation or LLC to buy properties in. This gives a level of protection from suit if a problem arises. Your accountant can provide you with the details on this.

4.   Time You are going to need time to research your target area, look at target properties, coordinate your renovation and market/advertise your property for rent. Most all of these activities can be performed after normal business hours. The only one that must be performed during the week is the closing when you must be present at the title company to sign all the papers, make sure to have your realtor there with you to oversee everything on your behalf.

5.   Hard money lender. This is an individual or company that specializes in loaning money on real estate. Rates are usually between 11-15 %. Most will charge a origination fee of between 1-3% of the money borrowed, see why we need to have some cash?

Advantages are hard money lenders will lend not only the amount needed to obtain the property, but also the money for the necessary repairs. Remember banks won't lend on a property that is not ready to occupy. Hard money lenders will not only look at your credit picture they will evaluate the property to see if a loan in the amount you are seeking makes sense to them. This protects you both.

CHAPTER THREE THE GOALS

When renovating our investment property we are concerned with four things.

1. Providing a comfortable, livable home for lease.
2. Ease of maintenance.
3. Obtaining a fair appraisal.
4. Resale value.

Let's set an example for ourselves and take this process step by step.

First we will need to determine our budget. This will be a function of how much we pay for the property and how much it should appraise for after renovated. Remember that we will only be able to get a 70% loan to new appraised value once the work is complete.

Therefore your realtor must do his job and you must do yours to make sure that the property that you would like to purchase will allow, based on the final price enough room for you to complete the renovation, cover some of the banking fees and some of the closing costs.

It is typical that some of your money will remain in the home. I'm not saying you can't recover all your costs I've been able to do this several times. I am saying don't shy away from a deal that will provide great cash flow simply because you left three grand in it.

So you've targeted a house you like and it looks like this, 1500 sq. feet, one story, brick exterior, three bedroom two baths with an attached garage.

CHAPTER FOUR: THE PROPERTY SEARCH

THIS CAN BE ONE OF THE MOST
FUN PARTS OF THE WHOLE
PROCESS. FOR THE PURPOSE OF
THIS EXERCISE WE WILL BE
USING AS AN EXAMPLE A ONE
STORY BRICK THREE BEDROOM
TWO CAR ATTACHED GARAGE.

When you begin you will want to have a few
resources available to you. A nice map of the
area you want to view. You will want to have a
flashlight as most likely the power will be off. And
a digital camera for taking photos that you can
save to a file. A note pad or tablet to record
notes.

When arriving at the target property, begin by walking around the outside first. Make sure to take a picture of the front as this will provide you with a visual reference for you file compilation. Now you're on the property, here are some questions to ask. Is the driveway on even? Are there cracks? Is the sidewalk lying properly? Or is it a hazard?

Is the property over grown? Are the trees overhanging the roof? Does the earth where the foundation meets it overlap? This could be a place where water enters the property or termites may enter here as well. Does the roof have any dips in it? How are the shingles? Are they broken? Curled? Stained?

Any of these issues will add to the cost of your repair estimate. That takes care of the front of the property; now let's go around the side. We will now be looking at the brick siding. Are the walls straight? This may sound funny, but I bought a home once where the brick was falling away from the interior frame. Are there cracks? This may indicate foundation failure, or if not very big it may just be normal settling. Are the windows broken? Are the doors in place? Are they still functioning?

They may need to be replaced. How about the air conditioning compressor or ac unit as it's commonly called. Is it old and tired looking? Is it even there? If it's old you may have to replace it. Again remember to look at the trees to see if they are overgrown and hanging too close to the roof as this can be a cause of major damage to the roof and as a consequence the interior as well.

As you observe the outside remember to take notes and pictures. I always have a spiral bound note book to write my notes and at the top of the page the property address. Commit one page per home at least so you do not become confused when viewing several properties at one time or session.

Oh and before I forget how did the wood trim near the roof look? Commonly called the fascia, was it intact? Or is it rotten? Does the paint look good? Chances are on an older foreclosed home the exterior will have to be painted. Remember if the home is older than 1978 you may need to refer to the govt doc# for lead based paint removal.

Now let's move to the inside. How does it smell? If you smell mold or see evidence of mold on the interior walls leave immediately. I cannot stress this enough. Black mold is dangerous and there is no reason to fool around with it. I once had a client who wanted to buy a home where the roof had been damaged severely and the price on the property was attractive.

My advice has been and always will be, do not buy these homes that have sever mold issues. If you do you must have a certified mold remediation specialist remediate the problem and he will then provide you with a certificate that the problem has been dealt with according to state law. This can be expensive but necessary.

I have walked away from several mold damaged dwellings. This also applies to fire damaged homes, the process of putting out a fire requires a lot of water and so almost without fail these home will have extensive remediation needs. It may be best to either do it right or not at all. Enough about mold.

Now were on the inside, let's look at the floors are they carpet? If they are they probably need heavy cleaning or to be replaced. Do the floors slope? If so this is a very good indicator of foundation work that needs to be performed. Unlike mold foundation problems can be remedied fairly easily.

All you need is a foundation company that warranties their work. See if their warranty is transferable this is important if you ever intend to sell the house, which one day you probably will.

Walls, are they severely damaged? If the home has been through an earthquake you can bet they will be. They may be cracked from normal settling in any regard we need to check to make sure the doors operate properly and the windows work as well.

Do the windows have blinds? You will need to provide blinds and screens if you intend to lease the property to anyone receiving a HUD voucher or other government assistance. While on doors, are there hardware issues? Are the door knobs in place? Are they painted over, or just plain ugly? In the next chapter we will cover making your property appeal to new tenants and also making the appraisal.

Let's now examine the kitchen. Are all the appliances there? Stove, dishwasher? Do they work? Are they too beat up and needing to be replaced?

You may provide a refrigerator, or you may not, this will be addressed in the chapter on making the home ready to lease.

The cabinets, do the drawers all work are all the cabinet doors remain? Your contractor may need to rebuild some of these items. How about the floor in the kitchen? Is it vinyl? Or tile? If its vinyl chances are it will need to be replaced.

Let's move into the bathrooms. Are all the fixtures there? Sometimes you will find a vanity is missing or a faucet. Are the tub and toilet serviceable? If the tub is rotten and rusty it will need to be replaced and along with it the tile enclosure as well. And if you have to pull the tile off the wall you may as well replace the shower valve that meters the hot and cold water. Once you tile up that wall getting back behind there again will be an expensive problem.

Is the plumbing leaking? Are the mirrors cracked? Faded? Does the toilet flush? Take a lot of notes.

Bedrooms, you will find invariably that, closet doors are missing, closet rods are missing as well. Kid's rooms will sometimes be painted an awful dark color, mine was blue when I was a kid, how about yours?

Garage, this will typically contain the water heater let's make sure it's up to date and functioning.
After all the required repairs are preformed you will need to begin the lease process.

Begin by getting a lock box and attaching it on the front door. These can be had at any home improvement center for around thirty bucks. You will then need to place a sign in the front yard advertising the property for rent along with your or your manager's phone number. At this point you will have to start interviewing prospective tenants.

Make sure you are doing background checks and credit research to determine if your prospect will be a good renter for you. This part I like to sub out to my property manager as they do a complete job and will deal direct with the tenant. Remember that the property manager should have on staff a handyman that can fix any minor repairs that come up under 200.00 this keeps you free to focus on obtaining more rental properties for your portfolio.

CHAPTER FIVE: WHEN RENOVATING

When renovating a few key points will be discussed here. Try to fix all the little details that will drive your manager buggy if they are not addressed.

First we will need to repair all cracks in the interior walls and ceiling. Next we may want to paint the ceilings; I recommend that this is almost always done. Also paint inside the closets and garage to give the home a clean look. Check all water supply lines to make sure all leaks are taken care of. Check all electrical outlets' to make sure they are up to code. Almost all the homes I renovate do not have the proper GFCI type outlets that are required in all areas near by a water supply such as kitchens and baths. Fix any cracked or broken windows and install mini blinds. Paint the interior wall of the home eggshell finish for ease of cleaning.

I like to keep all my homes on the same paint scheme, with the same manufacture. This keeps repaints a breeze as well as touch ups. Try white ceilings, flat finish same for closet interiors and I paint the garages flat white as well.

For the walls of the home I use a common beige color and again white trim for all the base board, doors and cabinets. I once had an investor tell me that he never painted inside the cabinets on his rentals, really? That just sounds so unfinished to me.

Now that the messy part of painting is over we can focus on the flooring. Well a lot of investors I know opt for a complete tiled house. This is ok if you like I prefer carpet in the bedrooms. Yes every three years or so as tenants move out I have to replace it, but I think it gives the home a much nicer feel.

Each can decide for themselves. Tile will cost about twice as much as carpet. Some folks are going with a laminate flooring now which costs about the same as carpet. I don't recommend it for floors in wet areas such as kitchens and baths. I have seen it numerous times but if it gets wet it will fail, and if you purchased it from one of the big box retailers you probably won't be able to match it up, that goes for tile as well.

The big box retailers buy in huge quantities and are able to offer some great pricing as a result. The only problem is replacement. When you buy tile in this fashion buy ten or so extra tile and store them in the attic that way if there is damage you will be able to replace it with a match. Vinyl is fine in roll form for laundry areas baths and kitchens even. It holds up well and can be quite cost effective.

Just make sure the installer has experience as there are a few tricks to doing it right where it will last. Countertops, these can be Formica, which is also called laminate.

Or if you prefer you may install tile, this is my least favorite and doesn't seem to be to popular any more thank
goodness as the grout can become dirty and a germ trap.

 Let's stay with a solid surface product like Silestone or laminate and avoid the germs. Now about the appliances. We need a stove or range whichever is called for by the design of the kitchen. One of my investors hates wall ovens and if they need to be replaced he just rips them out and installs a range.

When I renovate I try to remain true to the way in which the home was designed as one day I will sell my investment properties and for that purpose I don't want to go back and have to spend money to get it back up to for sale condition by re installing what was there already.

If you have the time you can find almost anything on Craig's list so finding a replacement wall oven for a low cost should not be a problem.

When it comes to installing a wall oven or any other hard wired appliance call a licensed electrician, they will do it right and it will pass inspection when you sell the home in the future. While on the subject of inspections, if you are in a city where permits are required to so much as replace a toilet you will need a licensed plumber or electrician to perform the work and have it inspected. I always say nothing wrong with doing it right.

Let's also remember that the outside needs attention. Are the shrubs trimmed back? Let's make them presentable oh and if by the way there is any foundation work to be performed it has to be done in the beginning as there will be cracks and holes in the floor created by the process, don't worry the foundation people will fill those in, but if you already installed your tile it will be a major problem.

Make sure to cut the lawn and trim back the trees. Does the outside need to be painted? Remember that little detail of making a favorable appraisal.

While on the subject of appraisals a few tips. I always make a point of meeting the appraiser on the property so that I may personally answer any questions they may have. You don't always get exactly the number you want but it doesn't hurt to let him or her know what you have done to improve the property.

If you paid to have a property inspector look at the property than make sure that you are able to implement all his recommendations so that the property is up to code and safe for all to rent. Last but not least have the entire inside of the property cleaned and straightened out before you begin your showing process.

CHAPTER SIX: A TYPICAL SCENARIO

Let's say you have assembled all the necessary team members and tools. You are about to embark on your journey to becoming a rental property investor.

The following example will provide you with a road map to follow which you may alter as you like once you feel comfortable with what you're doing.

1.   Instruct your realtor to begin looking for target properties. Let's say you're in Houston and you want to stay within a 15 mile square geographical area to minimize travel time when you need to travel to the property. You may need to retrieve the sign from the yard after leasing or pick up a rent check or just drive by to see your investment, always a good idea.

2. View the property; you may want to accompany the property inspector as he performs his task, keeping in mind that an inspection on a small home can take up to three hours.

Make sure this listing entity has the power and water on so your inspector can check all the systems. The inspection should reveal any defects, and to be sure there will be some. Are there termites? Any other pests? Frame damage? Are the foundation, roof, and electrical up to code? Water heater functioning? What about the A/C unit? Is it even there? All will be revealed in the inspection report.

3.   Your GC can be there as well to give a preliminary estimate and final once the inspection report is finished. This can also be a negotiation tool if the repairs seem to be more than your cash flow projections can stand, you may ask the listing entity for a price reduction in accordance with your GCs repair estimate.

4.   Making an offer. When making your offer it is best to consider the cost of your rehab and any associated fees regarding the hard money loan as these are what's termed hard costs. Soft costs may be considered to be, permitting, plans, architectural fees if any are applicable. In addition other soft cost would be utilities bills and any miscellaneous costs. So, the asking price may be a little too high for all your costs to repair and finance.

Our goal is to be as close as possible to include all our costs in the 70% loan to value after our repairs are completed. You may lose a few along the way, or you may adjust your offer to allow for a few thousand to remain behind in the property. Positive cash flow should make this up in a year or so. If our renovation is done well, we should make the hoped for appraisal. Thus allowing for most, if not all of our cash to be returned to us at the second closing.

5.   Do not make an offer on a property that sits in a flood zone. The cost of flood insurance will obliterate your cash flow in almost all instances. Please stay away from food zones for rental property purchases.

6.   Purchasing the property we will be closing on the investment property in two phases. First phase will be the hard money close to get the project started. Second will be the take out financing that will allow you to mortgage the property for up to thirty years.
Make sure that all the fees and closing cost associated with the loans are as stated. I have found discrepancies at closing and had to have the documents changed on the spot.
Have your realtor there as well the can help you go over the documents as there are a bunch of them. That's where the realtor gets paid so they are going to want to be there any way.

Once you have closed the hard money loan the property is yours. You will want to begin the renovation process immediately as in the next day, remember you're paying 2 % on your hard money loan for the time it takes to rehab and refinance out so working quickly is important.

Place a lockbox on the property so all the trades can have access and you will not have to be there every day to let someone in. Obtain an insurance policy for unoccupied property from your insurance agent before work begins.
You must turn on the water and power for the process to move along, so this is one of the first things to do.

Some hard money lenders will give you a first draw to get started, some want to see some progress, come out and inspect and then give a draw.

Typically on a rehab of 20k or less they will provide two draws. My way is to have the first draw equal 50% this is usually enough to get through the job and then submit for a final draw once rehab is complete. Again this will come down to your relationship with your contractor and your lender.

So here we go,

Example 1

1. Purchase price	56,000.00
2. Cost of rehab	13,000.00
3. After repaired value	99,000.00
4. 70% loan to value	69,300.00
5. Less closing costs	4,500.00

6. Cash in deal   4,200.00

7. Rental income
4,400.00

8. Management and repairs
1,120.00

9. Note on home at 7%
4,830.00

10. Taxes
2,722.50

11. Free cash flow
5,727.50

This is meant to illustrate the potential of residential rental investments in the Houston Texas market place. Your actual results will vary.

Still I will let you calculate the cash on cash return. Looks pretty good right?

Once you begin the process you may want to add several more properties to your growing portfolio. As the rules stand currently you may own four properties in addition to your primary residence, as long as your debt to income ratio is good.

After you have reached the limit you may want to form an LLC to hold the properties as a business, this removes the five property limit. Your lender in most cases, will expect a little more equity in this instance.

This guide is meant to give you as the investor an overview of how to invest in the foreclosure market to yield cash flow. In addition with time you should also realize an equity appreciation to add to your total return.

Remember we are obtaining these homes at 55-65% market value. There will be times when the ratio will be lower say 45% that will provide a much greater cash flow as long as cost of rehab remains relative.

Let's look at a couple of more real world examples.

6215 Ridge Creek

This home was foreclosed and had a car crash through the front of the home collapsing the brick siding and damaging the frame.

1 .Purchase price
50,000

2. Cost of rehab
23,000

3. After repair value

108,000

4. 70% loan to value

75,600

5. Closing costs

4,500

6. Cash in deal

1,900

7. Rental income

11,700

8. Management and repairs

1,100

9. Note on home

5,292

10. Taxes

3,240

11. Cash flow

2,068

10381 Wilmore Lane

1. Purchase price
52,000

2. Cost of rehab
22,500

3. After repair value
103,000

4. 75% ltv
77,250

5. Closing costs
4,500

6. Cash in deal
1,750

7. Rental income

1,700

8. Management and repairs

1,100

9. Note on home

5,407

10. Taxes

3,090

11. Cash flow

2,103

Definition of terms

1.   ARV after repaired value. This is the value of the property after all renovations are complete. Here is a goal we are shooting for of 100% of appraisal

2.   Rehab. This is the process of renovating the property

3.   Comps. This term is meant to convey comparable as in rental averages, or in listing prices on property

4.   Hard money. A higher interest loan meant for a short term to renovate property.

5.   LLC limited Liability Company. A form of business entity meant to be used to hold your property investments.

6.   Closing. Formal transfer of real property, usually performed at a title company

7. GFCI ground fault circuit interrupter

In conclusion

I hope you will all find success in your investment property endeavors. There will be more learning experiences along the way and many joys as well.